I

c

o

p

e

ICON

Poems by
F. Douglas Brown

For Hermia and Fred...
my first examples of excellence.

CONTENTS

∾

"The source of any of my content in selecting Harriet Tubman, Frederick Douglass…was more of a self expression, and maybe seeing myself in these roles."

–Jacob Lawrence from Los Angeles County Museum of Art Artist Interviews (1993)

"…this man, superb in love and logic, this man
shall be remembered. Oh, not with statues' rhetoric,
not with legends and poems and wreaths of bronze alone,
but with the lives grown out of his life, the lives
fleshing his dream of the beautiful, needful thing."

–Robert Hayden from "Frederick Douglass" *poem (1966)*

"If only he be great in his line, he is an unfailing source of interest, as one of a common brotherhood…our chief desire is to know what there is in man and to know him at all extremes and ends and opposites and for this knowledge, or the want of it, we will follow him from the gates of life to the gates of death, and beyond them."

–Frederick Douglass from "Self Made Men" *(1872)*

Daguerreotype c. 1841

    someone must have paid for you
to sit still   handed you hard cash

    for a new haircut and striped silk
stock which must be blue or purple

    something regal to stiffen
the collar   what a collar indeed

    and what a vest and coat too   royal
pressed and dapper fit   the tailor

    must be as proud as your coif
sheen and oiled face   handsome

    honeyed eyes burn the edges
of image and   gawker   I have to look

    away   your behold says: *work
to be done   these streets have forgotten*

    what I offer—: this thick baritone
if paint can capture a small glimpse

    of you let it be skull and chin
bodice and grip   yes   your aura back

    in Black folks   in Harlem
a small band of us hold your *deep set* and

    dramatic visage   yes   fresh faced
dreamers—: with the potential of heaven

I. Begotten

Annunciation: Frederick Augustus Washington Bailey

after Mary Szybist

Fra Angelico, 1433-34, Cortona

Change the light and dove floating
      upon daggered rays. Gaze a bit, take in

the jungled lawn or gilded backgrounds. Hold space
      elsewhere: altar, staircase, monastery plaster, chapel—

to better orientate halos
      or overflowing gowns, this space deep

in southern heat, inescapable for generations
      heat, a free life unthinkable heat. Reconsider

distance, an angel addressing Harriot Bailey— not Mary.
      Hear and heed these announcements to Harriot's

chapped and aching slave hands, hands full
      of grace, close to grasping Gabriel wrapped

in the light of her likeness to dispel fear, shock, her
      cloistered breasts still wondering: *why me*?

What Lord? What work to make ready, set asunder
      and burn? What to prep before the boy arrives?

Botticelli, 1601, Florence

Do not run,
my intrusion—:
      not a violation
      but a warning

These lilies observe
opposites, containers for
    birth, for death,
        flowers so fleeting

I understand
shunning,
       back peddle—
       evading eyes

Working forever— what
this land provides:
    shameful commerce,
        people without leisure

Take my cape,
this veil for Frederick—
       protection for
       the unformed or unframed

Hail Harriot,
hail your hands:—
    blessed be your offspring,
    blessed be your duty

Hail Harriot,
the surprise
    your gaze pushes,
    gathering the answer: *yes*

Begotten :: February, 1818

Douglass Panel 1

Black runs wild in Talbot.
Runs like the river runs
Through water,
Runs like a child
Through childhood.

The women do chores
In the middle of this.
Do the bulk of black living.
They hold stars on their heads.
Call the gold, *grain,*
Or call the gold, *East.*
Call it, *ripe for the pluck*, or *safe
Passage.* Say, *make a move*,
And call it, *gone.*

So much black everywhere.
Ubiquitous on trees,
Grows in a buzz
On elbows, streaks
The reeds, and strides across
The plains. A crooked
Hand out of the sand
Black hand of God, *Save us.*

But the white men approach,
Holding what could be shovels
Or rifles. Trying to dig

Or shoot God gone,
Right out of sight.

And still, here is this
Baby, born unto this land
In these matchstick
Boxes, born unto the silt
As bold as black lighting
Or a tree. He's a quake,
Cracking the earth
From limb to limb.

Darkness, My Mother

Douglass Panel 2

My restlessness, from my mother.
Her gift to tell a tale into the wood & dirt
Feeds me for the rest of my life.

She cups gold for me, butter
Or could be a cookie, a coin for a ferryman.
Could be a canary or just a candle

To guide her. Twelve miles
Of danger, and back to danger. *Massa,*
I aint no fool, been here all along.

A lie worth the gamble, worth the luck.
She could disappear through
The seams, the boarded wall, and into

The nowhere of night.
But I've come to love the blue diamond
Darkness—her risk keeps these quarters

Taut. Her grip in the huddled light,
Only has a few glimmers left.
Corn bread, coated with sugar

Or just the corn. Might be a shirt,
Her name stitched across
The yoke I will grow into.

Go Fo'

1.
::   mom wasn't cooking
     all the ingredients were there

     use lunchmeat for tacos and tomatoes from last night
     use box cheese—*grated will do, it melts better that way*

2.
My mother, black knees matching her hair, black knees from field soil, spit and burn. Only eight, and in charge of three or four strawberry rows, each needing to be picked before July erupts, scorches the glossy fruit. Dreams of new shoes and school clothes drip from everywhere. Head to toe wet with hope, my mother picks the morning away, fills a satchel to the brim, shakes out the leaves.

3.
::   make a burger or fry some rice

     crackers slathered with tuna
     or late-night bologna, cold or butter burnt

     edge-water or kool-aid
     tampico or sunny-d to wash it

     and you down for the night

::   *do whatever or leave your belly*
     hollow, a dried canteen

     in a wasteland
     port, and its

     wind-hum:— your emptiness

4.

When she stops to wipe away her sweat, or stops for water, she can see her brother Danny and cousin Junior in the wavy distance. Both boys, bold as the plants they sort through, shirts off, skin ripening faster than the berries. They joke, make a game out of body punishing work. Youth, too eager in that sun and space for my steadfast mother. She locks her way. She steps on clumps of faces—two blocks worth of furrows and dirt faces keep her going: *Enday gets to stay in and cook. Noah and Ronnie are too cute for this. Their skin will spoil in this heat, Mom, says. And she's gone. Again; for the day or week, it doesn't matter.* My mother's young thoughts ache, but her back can feel the cling of a new dress.

5.

:: go-for-what-you-know
    buying church clothes and paying the collection, too—*gofo'*

    new chucks—*gofo'*
    picture money—*gofo'*

    tickets to school dances and away games—*gofo'*
    the bus rides home—*gofo'*

6.

Because her cheeks are kind when she smiles; because she's smarter than her spectacles; because at a young age she could make a stove glow new, her Uncles Monico and Fred and wives take a liking to my mother. On the verge of their own families, they each ask her for help on weekends. They all cook. They all dance to *black music* on the radio, or Uncle Monico on a jazz jumping saw. Its song— blocks mosquito bites, swings the flies to Satchmo, swoons to Lena Horne.

7.

::   a recipe for making your own
      way when mom couldn't help
      not doing a damn thing tonight, kids

      off duty feet, swollen tired
      a foot massage until she snores,
      rumbling the room clear

8.

The hills like a brown Kahlua pig, roasted bright with hot coals in a ditch, banana leaves and burlap. The pig will feed the entire lot of workers after outhouse and outside showers. My mother is allowed to stop and eat long before the boys who will grumble and call her names until they piss their pants. Her Uncle, his Filipino ears and leather switch, will catch the boys in the act; will smart their silliness and disrespect; will tan it clean off and into murmur, so my mother can eat. My mother, her limp cabbage body, slowly chewing tiny bits of meat and rice as the sun drops over the last pig.

What I Mean When I Say *Begotten*

The shifting winds of remembering riding the night you was born:—
Your daddy's rock-dumb expressions, drunk on the night you was born.

Your mama too sick to seek a hangar or harbor in that man.
She fought the fool in her. Rolled weight onto the night you was born

Rather then decipher your daddy's whereabouts. His garbled mess
Of words couldn't muffle the pain caused by the night you was born.

Any wave of excuses, any apologetic scats curling fast:—be his best
Al Green, imitated organ tones heating the night you was born.

Love & Happiness be a mouth full of Mississippi, be bad beer &
    hoochie-coochie.
Nonsense ran them streets and not into the hospital. On the night
    you was born,

Your mama, a sliver and a small ember hanging to the wind. Recovery—: a
Blood dance or coin flipping down a deep well. On the night you was born

She let the drugs kick, but wouldn't wait for your daddy's tears
And paper bag prayers to finally stumble into the night you was born.

She would punish his ass real good:—slapped his full name on you
To force love to burst longer than the night you was born.

Love gon' keep him present, Dougi:—This, the day you tell her your daddy
Is dead:—and how right she be forty years after the night you was born.

Re-Portrait as a Muslim Boy :: Beg. Borrow. Steal.

Beg

Go back to being 4 or 5.
Your mother serious
with a man named *Mulasim*, a Muslim
who taught you the ways of men
in a mosque, how to pray
with the whole of you while also loving sci-fi
or kung-fu. Mom and Mulasim,
so tight they changed your name
to Jamal Muhammad—
Jamal :: beauty in big curls
and smiles, *Muhammad* :: praise above
all others. With little connection
left to your own father or his
name or namesake—
how could you not want
these new handles?
Your mom tagged
the new moniker on all books,
a sort of marriage between her
and Mulasim, the man you would beg
for a nickname— *Mo* :: old world toughness
and fists at pronunciation to ward
off insults and blows
from your big brothers,
their names—kept, intact.

Borrow

What do you know of this boy,
         his used name— a rental, car or tux

What did he say at play-date, when his friend's
         blankness deciphered the length of *Jamal Muhammad*

What dreams whorled, his head
 tucked and prostrate in a room full of men

Did his 70's glam-&-sparkle know that
 people would later attack people in prayer

His fresh face and fro— a bull's eye for *hate crime*
 or *vilified worship* or *not your country*

Flash forward with this name still yours,
 this version— *Jamal Muhammad* all you own

Your life littered with miles of racial-ized
 lexicon— you hear the joke at open

You catch the stares your name pitches
 from blocks away

Possess this past :: *brave up* ::
 speak out :: *fight with*

So the name you borrow tattles long before
 any chance or explanation

When you are pulled over or pulled out
 of line in an airport, let this version peak

Repress code switch or wit rotating danger,
 shucking off fear— bear what this land forces onto so many

And let them stare into the beauty
 of the most praised one as you resist

Steal

:: the march upon wicked ways this land portends

:: away from harm, away from hunt and of course— hurt

::   a heartbeat snatched, unexpectedly

::   the life of a boy expires when relationship spoils

::   your mother crossing out every name she penned a year prior

::   replacing borrowed names with what you scrawl to this day

::   Doug Fresh, DJ Dougi-Doug, Dig Dug, Big Doug, Doug-the-
     dick-tease, Doug the dangerous, Douglas of dark water but weak
     ass kool-aide, Douglas— father of *fuck off* or *love you* dad

::   every version—: stolen

::   reshaping the vision of itself while traveling

::   roaming the world in search of peace

::   your name, paddling dark, slowly

::   rebirth happening:— this way, too

Re-Portrait Filomena with Harriet

after Ocean Vuong

Tubman Panel 18: Pre-Immigration Act of 1924

I.
Dream her face, here— muscle or just bone— stone
smirk, coconut oiled hair— thick, pulled to

a part— neat, black on the black of her
best blouse. Dream it ironed, then re-imagine it blue
with an orange bow, white lace neckline. Can color help

you see Hawaii :: brown and blush skin :: plush
fragrance in bloom— blue on orange?

Do whatever, but F. Douglas, you will never see
her hands. Like the photo's edge, laws exclude, cut off parts
that get sent back to spaces laws will later claim. You want her

to take a cigarette, smoke the clouded days away,
but fool, she is pregnant with your grandma. Step

back, watch— understand *strong* is more face than fingers.
How her gaze grips even as you fling her side-by-side
for icon comparison:— Harriet Tubman.

II.
Dream Harriet standing where Filomena's boat lands.
People piling out and scrambling onto a dock

before authorities tidal wave the wood clean. Good ol' Harriet offering
friendship, and a quick get away. Good ol' Harriet, one hand
supporting Filomena's belly, while the other, points toward

refuge— The Big Island. Your greats, Filomena and Froilan,
their haste riding with Harriet through haze and fog.

III.
Before you un-dream the quota that almost drowns
your grandma; before you let a law tear the photo tiny— check
the date tucked on the picture's corner. If it's one week

prior to your grandma's birth, let your mind conjure
plates full of pace and fear. If it's months—

F. Douglas, fully churn imagination
wild: grandma's early life with Filomena
replacing reality's cloud and shadow. Give

your grandma time. She will have many answers
if you ask. Don't be afraid— her help will hum this way:

Filomena means— friend of strength, means
she can carry Harriet's rifle. Look hard.
There's a goddamn blade of iron & maple resting

on my mom's hidden lap, loaded with thirteen elders
worth of light. Harriet means— rules the house. They share

the bullet-wish: kill, cleave or warn. For goodness
sake, Dougi, look at her. Your great grandmother rules
everything trying to destroy you.

IV.
O F. Douglas, don't wake up yet. Even while dreaming,
a grandmother is willing to say anything comforting

about her own. Let the ghosts play
fantasy and make-believe without an audience
to coax or caress with sighs.

What I'm trying to say, you already know—:
this one-on-one, never happened.

V.
Ode to braving on and beyond.
Ode to squaring your lip.
Ode to the lore a little boy makes

when he hears his grandma punched
out a man twice the size of a Redwood.

Ode to her John Wayne tongue high-riding—
to her horse tongue of slurs— to all the black men
she dated, and the laws she taught

your mother to break. Ode to the firm
of Filomena rolled through your grandma to
rest stubborn in your mom:— F. Douglas, they don't

play. Your mom, like your grandma, mowed
men and children down, slapping the sweet

cream out of anyone. F. Douglas, don't ever let
disarray enter your home. Ode to your grandma's
strong house. Ode to her white rice carpet— dream-soft,

until a spill broke the spell. Icons lined up
in her anger, waking you. And that part, real.

The Flogging

Douglass Panel 3

Colonel Lloyd make the babies watch

Colonel Lloyd try to break the babies,
      makes everyone watch

Colonel Lloyd beat Millie until the sunset
      so everyone see how a woman spirit get broke

Everyone see Colonel Lloyd

Everyone's eyes wide to the white

Wide as Colonel Lloyd's buck teeth

Everyone watch Millie tug at a tree

Everyone see Millie wrap herself around a gray trunk

Colonel Lloyd, red as the red, red as Millie's dress

Colonel Lloyd's red drips to the ground and muddies his boots

Everyone see Colonel Lloyd slip and Millie holdin' on

Hold on, girl, hold on

All the lights is on and his whip is glowin'

But everyone see the brilliance on the top of Millie's head

Everyone see Millie hold the hand of God in that there tree,

      And so do Colonel Lloyd

      And so do Colonel Lloyd

Re-Portrait :: Selfie
for Sandra Bland

The fragile shell
Of two brown eggs
Dot your eyes

Every photo speaks
To the hard and soft side
Of a black woman

Remembering you— easy
When your dependable
Shine breaks *cloud* and *reckless*

How different the mug
Shot from the rest
Of what we know of you

*

in a car: passenger—

in a car: driver—

in winter or fall:—
      at a restaurant with moon earrings
            or gray backdrop with crystal earrings—

      at home on the couch
            at work or on the way—

in spring or summer:—
            out of town or recently moved
               to a new town—

outside and driving—

outside and searched—
       and then, in jail—
            and then, in jail—

       and then, in jail—
            and then—:

crown tilt sideways :: straight up :: straight down :: crown tilt to corn rows & braids, extensions, too— *Girl, you so fly* :: crown to twists & crown to curls :: crown from a left or middle part :: crown in Farrah-Fawcett-70's-wave-&-bounce :: crown like necklines, V or crew or bra or strapless or tee— done fast on the move :: crown with someplace to be :: crown always watching :: always watching

*

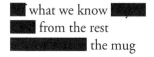 what we know
from the rest
the mug

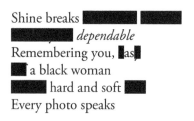
Shine breaks
dependable
Remembering you, as
a black woman
hard and soft
Every photo speaks

your eyes
brown eggs
fragile

Re-Portrait of an Icon
After McDuffie, Bright, Gustovich, Jackson, Young

> *Augustus Freeman IV aka Icon:*
> *Actually it's a symbol, something that stands for something else*
> *Raquel Ervin aka Rocket: Oh yeah. What do you stand for?*

Prelude

T- calls Douglass, *Superman*, man of steel-
   wool hair and wit to match. Courage, broad
     across his chest, fearless in the flight.

Imagine a Black Superman, someone announces,
   and we all play the game, play the fantasy
     out to our hoods and hot spots.

Imagine us—: the Boy or Girl Scout, the good deed
   in a cape, ungloved, no mask blocking
     skin— our open skin.

Icon#1 Departure

   Re-born out of ruin—:
Ruptured mechanisms. Starship wreckage.

   Re-born onto a DNA positive planet—:
Earth. America. Deep South. 1839.

   Re-born on the broke side of broke—:
Slave. African. Black.

   Re-born under a wide night—:
Universe and all its stars. My exploration, halted.

   The wide night and all its hopes in the form of—:
Slave. African. Mother.

Re-born to a black mother—:
Miriam. Loving me as her own. *Mothership connection.*

*

Prelude

T- calls Douglass, *Superman,*
       T- emphasizes Douglass's resolve, his *don't-give-fuck* ways
          T- underlines this into the air.

We play the game:— *Imagine a Black Superman.*
       We hold T-'s passion up with nods and sighs.
          What license does Douglass still warrant:—

Rizal, Ali, Zoot Suits, Parliament, hip hop,
       cultural wonder, hot breakfast, naturals, fists, beret?
          T- underlines this into the air, and we nod.

Icon#6 Chamber Light

       The room with blue
Light surging from my palms

       Cloud of blue to show my scowl—
I ain't playing lit everywhere

       The energy cracks blue, causes
My cape to climb, to sweep the light

       Blue air— the only wind and only
Light in this chamber, I wield

       So when I say, *Let her go,* the blue
Sizzles— light punctuates my command

*

Prelude

T- calls Douglass, *Superman,*
          And where are the women in this recollection
                  When does *super* equal all that a woman is

Play the game so *super* is redundant in her hands: Rocket.
          She bends metal, and learns to fly or fight, fast.
                  Learns her energy can heal as well as destroy.

What do you stand for, Rocket asks. Superman or Super Black
          Icon? What do you know about sacrifice and shadows?
                  About the margin? About holding a universe in your body?

Icon#8 Recollection

:   through sepia, through trees

:   into nightfall escape, into Underground Railroad thresholds

:   and departure, and a pack of dogs at my heels

:   civil war teeth, but reconstruction slow, lingering

:   is a graduation snapshot with family flanking the years

:   is an immortal's curse: family deaths pile up as do the years

:   asks: *just what am I fighting for,* and ponders: *by-your-own bootstraps*

:   has a dream, but avoids any oppression, for decades

:   has riches, and avoids any oppression, for decades

:   these snapshots, when confronted, when called out
          and made the foolish alien

:   when someone is impatient with power not serving the people

:   when someone knows an Icon can save the world

:   when an Icon should stop playing the game, and become
                 an example of humanity at its best

Your Name, Nobody
after Geffrey Davis/Robert Hayden/Yusef Komunyakaa

When memory can't recover
Any-which-way; when memory
Won't linger through— to bone,
To ache, the unforgettable;

When memory shifts about, towards nothing,
Dismissal, erasure— mostly your own.
Scant memory, no strike or sulfur,
Only a slow recline of vision— here

Amongst dust, amongst worn marble,
Reduction. Where is Miss Vangy,
Surely Her Sunday biscuits, golden
Fluff, baked love and syrup can kick

Or spark? Surely, your grandma's grand
Entrances, loop triumphantly, her red
For luck? Her sweetness, gone
In a puff or wish with nothing to leaven

Or leave behind for your children?
What fleshing lives need clinging to
When your name is etched on the wrong
Wall? Your name, nobody, *not worth*

A candle, your pop would say when comparing
Ball players. What are you chasing?
A daydream of smoke or history,
Memory's manipulation?

Your name, far from the work
Frederick Douglass manifested,
The reason you stiff-arm
His icon. You cleave the ironwood

Planks of his name. Damn responsibility
And damn the treads of lift, load,
And toil. Liberation— a remote and a couch.
Freedom— a channel guide lining up

Documentaries. Devour the details
And google the haste. Speak
From the rafters of social media. That will save,
Lead someone out of danger, right?

Brother, you have much to learn.
Remember your hunger— your real
And actual hunger. The real and actual
People— dying, while you forget who you are.

A Slave Boy's Lullaby

Douglass Panel 4

Momma say sleep, & then she go away
She say sleep, in my dreams she stay

O stars guide her through the black-black
O good Lawd, help her so massa don't lash her back

Fire on my feet, gon' keep the cold out
Gon' keep cold out 'til massa start to shout

Colored folks, share all we gots to give
Give massa our blood, jes so we live

Momma say sleep, so she can run away
She cant let her boy keep her in delay

O stars guide her fast, all through the night
O good Lawd, gets her home without any strife

Massa keeps his eyes on her when she sneak
Eyes always on her bres, he cant even blink

Momma turn her cheek, massa thrust, whine and wail
Momma make massa sleep so she can see her chile

Momma say sleep, and she be out and away
Gotta return soon, massa up in the day

O stars cover my face when she leave this slave cabin
O good Lawd, get her home quick so nothin'll happen
Jesus say he comin, he comin in a hurry
Comin to take my troubles, but so many to carry

O lawd, kill massa quick so momma can live in peace
O lawd, kill massa quick so momma can live with me

Second Sleep

the best kind of rest—somewhere between
deep drunk slumber and an afternoon nap

second sleep   when the body is
complete   lost in itself

when the body   defenseless with no
need except refueling   my son and daughter say

I'm the king of second sleep during movies
especially   they catch my heavy breaths in a net

of laughter or pointing fingers   they predict
the path my head will teeter during the trailers

O children of the dozing dad   recall
the number of naps when you each were

small melons   recall the repose
of your curling posture in my thick arms

my thumb praising your eyebrows
and forehead   your baby skin   your hand

around my pinkie as I move   gripping
solid as in—safety   as in—safety

as in—I take it back—:   that recollection
the best rest ever

II. The Beautiful, Needful Thing

Daguerreotype c. 1843

Circa July

>wavy high heat
>in my hair
>
>curls for a girl
>named Rosetta   and two boys
>
>Lewis Henry and Frederick, jr.
>their names—: stars
>
>and fireworks
>guiding me by night
>
>to safe passage   faster
>than a horse by day
>
>my children's laughter free
>to romp and gallop
>
>and so   I proceed

Circa August

>my shoulders slump
>from this freedom
>
>the weight for a runaway
>picks up wind and worry
>
>*how to help* fires off
>my tongue   everyday this
>
>month I will call
>out until a slave answers
>
>*here I am*

Circa 1843

the year of the 67th
Independence Day   what do I have

to commemorate   Liberty is
my white shirt and black overcoat

covering my flayed skin
slavery's fingerprints etched onto

me refuse forgetting—: I am only
recently freed   and memory

shackled by this sham

Circa Syracuse

I am less than two trains
and a boat away from my Baltimore

slave quarters but might as well
be on the Overland Trails searching

for Oregon or the hills of Scotland
or in Ireland doing a gig or hunting

pheasants   distance will not detour
or distract my doings   not a noose

nor leather strap will keep me
held   my tongue has the will

of my back   my tongue stirs
the sea of thousands   someone will join

my gaze   this steadfast stare moves
toward you brothers and sisters

I am coming to get you all

Planation Tour :: how a painting happens

Douglass Panel 5

I am choosing to walk up the trail
leading up to the big house, choosing to visit,
to see what would not have been privy to me

a century ago. The house, amongst the boughs of trees
and mossy green, is a white brighter than the sun.
The white shimmers white, shimmers staircases

on both sides. They spread the way wings
roll out, or like how the old film reels that hold
the image of this place unravels and lolls— all ages,

throughout the ages find this place, easy. The staircases
are open arms to all that visit. And that's why, after all
these years, the haints still hover. It's why the slave

cabins in the back could hold a platoon. Flocks of pigeons
still roost and cane grows up into your nose
for miles down the delta. The columns are formal,

doric the guide explains. A double chimney
to match the fine craftsman's symmetry. Two hundred
years of ancestry cover the bricks. At every step,

I am reminded that this was *small* in comparison,
a joke until I am in a *massa's* bedroom:
Here the grand gallantry perfumes the air.

Here rugs match the mirrors. The wood polished
to a high buff, keeps the room lit. There is blue
everywhere— the blue creased sheets,

and a blue bed curtain with embroidered birds
spurting away. Here, a gold rope is not for lynching
yet is still braided to the slaves out back.

There is a white doll asleep in a crib, tucked in
the warmth freedom and luxury afford.
But what halts me helpless—: red tulips dying

on a mantle. Their nobility contained in a vase,
and flailing about unnoticed. Their arms raised up
to heaven, pleading: *Get me out, dear Jesus. Get me out.*

Up Jump the Funk Never Felt this Bad

after John Murillo

Douglass Panel 6

Captain Auld will try to shake,
try to rattle and roll, he'll try

to sweep and shake
his cruelties into a crack,

oversee and shimmy-sham
with the best of them.

Captain Auld will try to
breakdance, even in 1825.

Bust a backspin on his
slave, shined floor.

Clean it again, and again,
         dip dip da, dip dip da
                  til I say it's right!

In one shoulder-pop
and teeter, he will try

to cabbage patch, put a lash
across your ass, make you

quarrel on his behalf,
who's massa better?

Captain Auld will try to tip toe
off, then moon walk, or cowboy

in his green hat. He will jerk,

hustle, and do some Kung Fu

fighting. His hand raised, big boss style,
fast as lightning, might chop your life

right out if you disobey,
if you try to think on your own.

Boy, I will claim the hell
out your future. I be damned
if you learn how to read.

So when you hide, behind his wife,
you already have bushels

of books and stacks
of pamphlets to read, hidden

from Captain Auld's
wicked boogaloo.

You already you know
not to look his way.

No telling what you
might see. No telling what

itch your folks will catch later
down the line.

Olemrauldsaythisthegospeltruththatifyouteachthatniggertoreadtherebenokeepinghimandthaswhutmakemeworkiworktowriteandtoread: a ghazal

"O-bour   mo-bouths   bo-broke   the-bem/ a-band   o-bo-pe-bened the-bem/ fo-bor   ai-bair   o-bor   wa-ba-ter-ber/ o-bor   see-beed   o-bor foo-bood./ A-banse-se-bers,   que-bues-tio-bens,/ na-bames,   se-be-cre-bets." –Robin Coste Lewis

Douglass Panel 7

Ole Mr. Auld said, *if you teach that nigger to read
there be no keeping him,* so I became determined to read.

I saved biscuits and jam for the poor white boys, traded a piece of pork
for pencils and paper, or a lesson on cursive or a story read

aloud by someone who knew the correct pronunciation.
Sometimes I'd sing a bit, lull them to nap so I could read

an extra passage or poem. I could feel my stars alter their path,
a grand achievement evolving. To write is to fill my belly; To read,

is a pail of coal I can throw onto a fire deep inside me.
My heart burns through page after page. Read-

ing to the sunrise was not wise, but the risk was what I knew.
Like my mother, I only have a small torch to guide me. When I read,

I cover her hideous twelve miles. By day, I hide books in holes,
brush the dirt off every night. Most of the time, I am alone, read-

ing to myself. Frederick Douglass, how spoiled you are to have a weapon
of this size, concealed. Freedom on my face radiates with each word I read.

Why I Read: Partial Pecha

after Terrance Hayes

Douglass Panel 8

[Empty Shelves]
Small black words, stronger than all my muscles combined, idle on this forbidden height. My capturers keep a shelf full of books out of this slave's reach. The mere mention of owning words, could kill me.

[The Aloe in a Vase]
Little aloe, you're a paperweight, green flicker or tabernacle holding two hours of sacred talk— "Yes." I water you with the best-made tongue in the land: spittle as I attempt pronunciation. Soon you'll rise high, to see what I have in store for these folks.

[Table with Wide Legs]
Take me there, brother. Show me how to heave the load when fight kicks you in the teeth. Show me how to let grace walk across my back when it is pinned to the wall. How steady the reading. How sturdy the lesson.

[Columbian Orator]
This script, these tangled lines, the out loud truth they bear. Might bring death. Might be a bloody mess before the day strikes the window. So, Douglass, don't you dare tell a soul. Keep this between rest & daybreak, weeds & worry, between the Queen's speech & a slave's unsullied tongue.

[Wooden Walls]
We wade   We witness   We hold the hands of a boy greater than a thousand flocks put together   We be his pulse, youthful sternness   We his loyal beads dripping off our wooden faces before pooling on the floor   We huddle tight so there's no peeking between the cracks   No light to tattle

[Three Books]
Collecting coins, slow as gathering tears or July rain, but when you're
accustomed to nothing, anything turns dust to gold. Shine shoes by
day— then sneak to buy a book. Shine sentences by night— eat as
much as any one page offers. Then go back for more.

[Pot on a Bed]
Ode to the seasoned tongue full of options. Ode to the metal war
torn shield and helmet and not bed pan— piss & vinegar, bull shit &
such. Lift my iron heavy burden, clear my weighted down ignorance,
thick char and soot. Let every new word reveal my fish fry ambitions.

[Steady Left]
To steady the way I gather words off a page, I force myself to read
upside down. Inverted letters, like rain in reverse, pouring up to
quench and create a thirst I never knew existed. *Columbian Orator*,
the storm and flood that follows, my left hand tethered to each its of
free words, an entire pool of settled water. I dive deep.

[Candle Stick Prayers]
Let there be illusion, light to dispel what work & whip bring — Let
me cleave with a pencil the way I chop wood, ready for winter —
ready, when impossibility rocks me complacent, when

light is only a speck buzzing in my ear, let golden pages lift me, elbow
up — Let the flame burn words into my dark eyes, my damn dark
eyes.

[Marble Black Eyes]
Every new word tucked into the pocket of my mind is moon and
marble and barbell and baker stones and dream hoop and coffee cup
and the grounds, too and boot heel and belt buckle and canteen and
key hole and cosmos and cycle and wheel and pulley and pipe and…

and…

and…

Mr. Covey, Shall We Dance?

Douglass Panel 10

I am an ox, bare chested,
   no shoes, toes dug into
      the dirt, pants hiked up
         to my knees.

I can spell *rhinoceros* backwards,
   bend iron with my
      teeth and work the leather
         that breaks a horse in two,
            that breaks the blue of night
               into black— I am that bold.

I am the nails holding
   uneven boards upright.
      I will not splinter or buckle
         the soft wood nor will I yield
            to treachery, your evil ways.

Checkered devil, if you hold
   a hammer, then I'll hold your arms.
      One cinched at your hips, the other,
         high enough to twirl
            you around this barn, and to then
               to Japan (yes, I know of that place, too).

If this were a jig
   our glances might mingle,
      might be engulfed by sweat.
         We might be kissing.
            We might be juicy to floor,
               mud, logs, grass and more juice.

Combat's intimacy, close enough
    to see the red thread in your eyes
        or stroke the odd rough, the white
            bark of your skin.

As it is, the ax at your feet says, you aim
    to kill me. You wish to keep
        your reputation intact but you
            are stunned by this feat

of resistance. The shame blurs
    your vision. We wrestle like this
        for two hours, but for the rest of my
            life, no one beats me again.

Kundiman Beginning with Funk and Frederick

after Patrick Rosal/after Parliament

Douglass Panel 11

Parliament on the good foot
        kicks back to slave days

Bewilderment on the one
        [*Good God*]: Christmas

Or New Years when massa
        drew first blood with bourbon

And not a belt— corn, and not leather.
        [*We gon' turn this mother out*].

Dark spirits down a slave's dark throat.
        And now some slap boxing,

And now plenty of feet and eyes climbing
        to a rafter of stars or black nails—

The whole barn up on the down stroke.
        [*Ain't nothing but a party, y'all*]

Glad to be at rest, no dogs breaking
        skin at his heels—

Douglass sits still, grabs dirt
        with his toes.

"Boy, if you ain't gonna drink or dance,
        come over here and let's scrap."

Bewilderment hits crescendo:—
        this is when the kundiman begins.

[*If you hear any noise, it's just me
        and boys— hit me*]

Love— brawl and butcher funk,
        curse funk, I-can-make

Someone-bleed funk. Love watches
        Covey buckle on repeat.

Love hears the story ricochet,
        until it hits:

"Scrap, boy—
        I ain't Covey."

[*The desired effect of funk
        can move and remove, dig?*]

Praise be [*a whole lot of rhythm*] and
        tambourines, a few bottles

Turn their eyes up to heaven.
        Praise be [*a real type of thing*]:—

Douglass will not oblige their charms.
        His plans intact and waiting

Somewhere far from the overseer's drunk
        leer, the overseer's deadly dare.

Douglass and his thoughts,
        amen like chimes,

Amen through the love light—
        wave in gold and green.

Flight: — Determinate

Douglass Panel 12

Plans writhe
the mind and then out to
  air—: lashing

Air browns
ears—: huddled close
  brown bodies

Bodies full of spicy
dreams and daring—:
  freedom looming

Freedom, a message across
a slave's chest they read—:
  in secrecy

The danger of
misinterpretation could
  mean—: lashing

Whip sting and anger
keeps brown bodies
  attention—: stiff

Douglass keeps the boon
golden—: feeding bodies golden
  with hope

Hope is a thing in overalls
hair parted to the moon—:
  shifting eyes

Spark this plan to light the blue night

Black branches pointing north

A lone tulip speaks the will of God

Flight—: Contained

Douglass Panel 13

I am a tulip seeking the will of God

Black chains rein in my escape, chains

Spark fear into slaves, spark horse laughter, too

Shifty eyes:—
moon black on white faces
overalls and cropped hair shackle us tight

A while ago, we were
golden, wild with hope. Now, only boon,
reduced to black ink on a treasure-song poster:

$100 REWARD: RUNAWAYS! THREE NEGRO
BODIES AT LARGE— ALL SIX FEET HIGH WITH
ANGER SCARRED BETWEEN THEIR EYES—

LASH AT WILL: BEWARE— THEY
COULD BE CHARMING— MUCH
OF THEIR INTELLECT— EXTREMELY DANGEROUS

Secrecy:— measured in months
read[justing]:— in the miles stretching
across brown land while whites mock my

Freedom, my steps, my
daring attempt:— reduced to dirt and
spicy dust, cloud-cover for our broken

Bodies. We so damn
close they resort to using our own
brown faces to stomp our conspiracy

Air, free air, close enough
to cling to a dream— close enough to ring or
writhe *any* necks trying to stop us: white or black

Free Hymns

Douglass Panel 15

I am a sailor
I am a skif
Jetting across the black stream

Sail me without selling me
Send me into legend
I am free

Not a Bailey
Not a Johnson
New York will take me as I am

Just man with swollen hands
Tired fingers, dirty and cramped
But free

She is there to cling on to my courage
There to bear fruit
We grow and gather together

A bag of potatoes or roots of good fortune
Ours in matrimony
Free to eat or share

The sky is kind, watches with warmth or with rain
Rinse the dust and heal my bruises
There are marks that will not dissolve

Indented pain will pass on to my kin
I can be a friend to my blood again
Free to hold him tight into me

I am of the isle and lake
Douglass by day
Douglass by night

Douglass the safe water
Gathered in a bay or a bottle
The responsibility of freedom inked in my name

III. All Extremes and Ends and Opposites

Annunciation: Barack Hussein Obama II
after Mary Szybist

> *I was able to drink…*
> *I took it [apple brandy; spirits] because it made me feel*
> *I was a great man…I used to think I was a president.*
> *–Frederick Douglass*

St. Priscilla Catacombs, late 2nd Century, Rome

Hints of apple brandy hit, and I am
a haint, Prophet ghost— an archangel.

Hail my mind's moral liftoff— hail my flippant posture
snubbing gravity— it's not the liquor, this must happen

Roaming forward— Kansas, then islands.
Long past border and county lines, I sail west.

Hail swig or toast, a shot's sting— black
outlines your belly's potential

I sail the freedom stream, air in my teeth
and tweed, my graying hair— until I reach her.

Rejoice Ann, full of grace, I am nothing to fear
or run from— Rejoice as the favorable one

Stunned into the purest blank, without worry,
her face, so bare upon my baritone.

Rejoice rule breaker, hail lawless, hail love; slander
and judgment turn you into: mother

Miscegenation laws keep her hands despondent,
but not deaf— a Kenyan sings his name to her.

My name, God strength, take it for protection, take it
for the turbulent road ahead

Chair and recline— again, I am someone ready
to deliver *divine*, ready to touch earth, shake it down.

My name, peaceful ruler, my pose never
touches you, but history leads your path

I was a great man, but what dances in her
womb, the world waits for— Rejoice.

Poem My Mother Doesn't Want Right Now

      my mother down the hall fast   like a train
or a bus blurting away   her sprint turned

      to tears:— and then into drops
of shit   a trail of shit and she

      is a paper icon   is bread and dirt
crumbling in the murderous hands of the hall

      I try to scrub fast   fast as my mother's leap
into the bathroom and into embarrassment—:

      soiled gown   closed door   tears to
the ceiling   thudding between the fan blades

      am I right saying nothing   letting this slide
off the now clean tile   pine disinfecting

      the moment   am I right as I quietly wash her
clothes   erasing the residue of what age is doing to her

Un-Portrait of Frederick Douglass

Everyone got high levels of entitlement in our veins.
—Morgan Parker

I sever my name and hell still breaks
my dead father. My move away
from his name, not a move

away from him, but from you,
lion eyed icon. What little
I have earned being a "Frederick."

Distance from pain
Leathering my back or knees—:
I buckle at traffic, long lines

of coffee drinkers at a café,
or the rude woman on her phone
in the store, *so damn loud.* I am far

from your anguish bending planks
for white folks so they can live
right, but also far from the boy

who grew up in a one room matchbox.
We drove out the roaches
but couldn't stop the rats

or San Francisco housing hikes:—
public housing requests,
those deadlines, circled blood

and scribbled prayers on calendars
alongside birthdays. Maybe the isolated "F"
was for "fight," the temperament

a scared and broke boy takes
on when the odds have beady eyes
that scatter when the lights "flick."

"F" for "food fabricated" out of thin
boxes our church delivered to us.
"F" for food stamps or for tacos (I know

that doesn't start with "F" but fuckin'
good does). "F" for freezer-burned memory
because I just hung up the phone

with my sister and we cursed
our sick mother into a fine
paste, *who the "F" does she think she is?*

"F" for the privilege I "force"
"fling" "forge" :—
"F" for "forgetful" :—

"F" for "frequency" (and the lack
there of):— "F" for all
the "flavors" I will miss

when mom's body calls
"finished" before she's ready,
when her strength no longer "formidable."

At this rate I will only be able
to say "failure" "frail" "feeble" "frayed"
and it will mean me:—

not her, not my father,
and Mr. Douglass,
definitely, not you.

Anthem Kundiman: Work
after Patrick Rosal

Douglass Panel 16

            North begets safe
        labor with coals—:
a char so black they crack blue.

            I feel rocky beauty
        as if carrying pieces
of me for night,

            For caves shielding
        runaways. O mysterious
shine, I am your jet and sable

            cradled by a bright bird,
        flight to the edges. This body
of blue— dearest Anna,

            her deep patience keeps me
        steadfast. Even though
I sleep with a shovel,

            my hand reaches
        for Anna. She is freedom—
wide as a wharf,

            or the clipper
        it harbors— wide as the heat
the coals bring

            to white folks. Heat
        helps the day drift and doze—
but I never will.

Sermon in Nantucket: Garrison Commissions Douglass

> *"I will not excuse; I will not equivocate;*
> *I will not retreat a single inch; and I will be heard."*
> *-William Lloyd Garrison*

Douglass Panel 17

I speak from a distance to these pink and gray heads.
Will and faith lead them to a blond Jesus, and yet, I am here in between.
Not to distract or coddle— my *astonishing* words bell, beckon and
Excuse none for this predicament, slavery grips us all.

I invite you to this service, to let your vision rise from its plight.
Will you join this brigade? Will you offer your experience as guide so that
No congregation, no man, woman nor child has to fear lash or lord?
Equivocate nothing. The truth of your scarred back says enough.

I believe the narrative you have to share will cause trouble, and
Will cure the skin snatched off your bold body— I welcome both occurrences.
Not just whites and not just blacks, you will burn all ears, none will
Retreat from your testimony. Sir, I am no prophet. I am not
A soothsayer, but I see what springs fourth when you utter but a
Single phrase. It is music packed into a small stone.
Inch by inch, moving toward Goliath and striking true. Deliverance

And sheer grace. Not all angels fly. Some need persuasion to lift
    beyond this place.
I, like you Mr. Douglass, was named Misfortune and Fatherless at birth. So,
Will you help me help them to reconsider their conditioning?
Be the candle in a window piercing through the darkest of winters. Be the lark
Heard from on high, shackled only to freedom's sweet, sweet song.

Imagining Lawrence Imagine the 11th of August 1841

Douglass Panel 18

I want the gold of Douglass'
first daguerreotype, the frame

holding a frayed image—: pocked and near
crumbled if not for this gold rim

or gold in his skin, recently free
and glimmering. Can my brush strokes

match his spry 23 year-old tone? I think
not. Shall I paint a series of overcoats and top hats,

red and green hoods, blond hair galore? Should I capture
eyes and mouths, the expanse of blue

sky lyceum caught in their gaze and gasps
as they walk away: *such intellectual power-wisdom*

as well as wit? The astonished must be seen reveling
in a run-away slave's eloquence. *The Liberator*

gave Douglass luster in his speech before
any image, but I will make shine spill

to his shirt, and to eight panels thereafter.
Let the gold be the light of fine tuned words

and ways. Let it be the glory of summer, the heat
lifting as a leader is being birthed amongst a sea of pink.

Yet, I know hate is a brilliant color in and of itself
even there in Nantucket. So paint a boy

in a white tee, alone with his skepticism closest
to Douglass' grandstand and grand

gestures. This little boy:— hands on his hips, legs
braced and firmly rooted in a white

power stance. He is all hate planted
in rich soil, blooming fledgling

of things to come—: things the 20th century and beyond
still bring to black folks. Douglass, let your cape

dangle, and boots march the hill behind, beat your gilded
chest, and roar until you swoon. Let your first public

words point toward the rebirth of Harlem, a future
poised with my name on it. But kind sir,

whatever you decide to do:— fuss, fight,
or flee, keep an eye on that boy.

We : Endangered : We
after Douglas Kearney

"We-be   bo-broke   e-bev-ry-by/ sy-byl-la-ba-ble-ble" –Robin Coste Lewis

Douglass Panel 19

We shall overcome
We shall overcome
We shall overcome
We shall overcome,
somed-
We shall overcome
We shall overcome
We shall overcome
We shall overcome,
somed-

When club hits,
When sticks hurt,
When fists fly & knees find cock,
        stoned and yanked—:
We shall over protect,
We shall defend.

Endangered species — Endangered we

We shall overcome
We shall overcome
We shall overcome
We shall overcome
We shall overcome, somed-
We shall overcome, somed-
We shall overcome,
somed-

Hit 'em with the bop gun &
still they bring more:— eyes, hats, black jacks
hate our black skin,
hates our black minds more.
And that's when clubs flex,
thumps— bricks upside
our damn-dark heads.

80

Endangered species — Endangered we

Deep in my heart
I do believe
We shall overcome,
someday

If the blue didn't get us over the hump
they would wipe us off this clay mound.
I turn my hand loose and it stays swollen
    for the duration of my life,
I limp (not for kicks).
I use syllables, take up collecting canes
to keep me upright, and dangerous, hunted.

Endangered species — Endangered we

Why I Write: Partial Kucha
after Terrance Hayes

Douglass Panel 21

[Hair with a Right Side Part]
O Lawd, find me in the field
I'm servant to these papers, servant to dark ink, a servant to my blood
O Lawd get me

O Lawd, find me in the field
I know how to work hard, how to bundle and hall, I fissure the soil
O Lawd stand me tall

[The Aloe in a Vase]
Inspiration grows thick into testament— how out of nothing, beauty becomes fleshy, pulp green stem & stalk, story and scripture— little plant, you with me since the beginning of words.

[Umbrella and a Cane]
We be the swan and the golden goose   We be ready for storm or the Southern sun   We be feathered in black or skinned with clipped wings poised for a fight   We be head turned and in tandem, swimming in the lake where justice was baptized

[Magic Curtain]
You make me a wizard with words, self taught conjurer with eager sparks on dark.   Golden polliwogs in shaded water. Commas or crescents, I write to that murk—: the vast troubles of slavery stretch to the floor

[Window with the Blue Sky]
First, my speech, and out the window, to the distance, to longitude, to a vice as old as alcohol. I am a mule, a bull, a shaman, angel, wheel and cart, a superman— anything built to withstand leash and lash.

[Book Shelf]
Brother shelf, your paint matches my skin. Your thickness and my hard
head tell me times are changing. We are both called to balance the light
and a stack of books the size of impossible.

[Gold Buttons]
We more than these rags, this scant wardrobe has no stock on our
souls, our intellect or bodies. My gold links only accents. Their twinkle
won't protect either. The written— the only armor to ward off ropes
and chains.

[Overcoat Outlined]
How many names to write you right, Mr. Van Buren, Old Kinderhook,
the OK President, Little Magician, back room compromiser, wannabe
aristocrat. Your dandy, perfumed whiskers keep me in caricature, buck-
eyed terror or error— I know every word I write or say.

[Shirt, Tie, Waistcoat]
I dress the role
:   as fugitive, but somehow— the *happy* or *jolly* negro, rings out, lingers;
:   fabric, not fabricated news away from Garrisonian— I leave to destroy
      slander;
:   and *The North Star*, guiding work, helps undo what centuries have done
      to us;
:   with masthead motto, "Right is of no sex - Truth is of no color -
      God is the Father of us all, and we are all Brethren."

[Red Feather Pen & His Pointing Right Hand]
Red brings brother and sister presses together:
Freedom's Journals, The Rights of All,

The Colored American, Mirrors of Liberty,
Provincial Freeman. We share our blood work,

Blood-lined articles to write the red, to write spirit, and
Write the toil. We have so much work to do.

Camera Obscura: to Don Cheadle as Frederick Douglass

after Drunk History Vol. 5, 26 May 2010; Headley & Reed photo, 31 October 1894

You must have patted
your fro fifty times before you started

      filming that day, and yet the boof remains
tall to the door. The part in this hair of

      yours has jokes written to the skin, splits
emancipation with hair grease.

      Later, your 'do will white
into an arrow over a million viewers

      will laugh at. A million more won't
understand how an actor can spoof

      an ex-slave— *there just shouldn't be any joking
around with him. Him*—:

      self taught fugitive, Douglass, the sermon
for Lincoln. Douglass, broad shouldered

      nerve beaming into every slave's yearn
for freedom. Yet, you must think Mr. Douglass

      would appreciate this gag? You think
the stone and lion of his visage would crack

      into joy the size of peaches? Do you fancy
him the *happy slave*, with *kind and amiable*

expression, or the happy negro, all buck
and watermelon, all giggle and content?

O Don Cheadle, you know we are quite
serious and lovely folks. Make me believe you

curse distortion, bring me miles ahead
of your industry's gaze, its blind misrepresentation.

Show me how to trust talent,
and its keen handling of Douglass's profile.

All proper care extends beyond
six minutes and twenty-three seconds. Not Shadrach,

not Whitaker nor Richard Dreyfus has the skill
to free the already free. Tell me your

lip-synched genius is more
Headley & Reed, their 1894 photo

where a proud and accomplished
aristocrat sits old and upright, thick fall

coat over a smartly starched shirt, crispy white
matching his mien or to match the snows

soon to arrive, Douglass and his last winter
gaze toward the future:—

DuBois, Harlem Renaissance, Malcolm,
Martin, Miles, Aretha, Nina Simone.

He's gonna love James Brown, Hammering
Hank, Jordan, Mae Jamison, the Obamas,

any and all between, too:
you, me our seed, sparks of what's to come?

Don Cheadle, does your depiction capture
clarity? Will your portrayal lift him to the real

and tangible, when an admired icon
pops off history, and permits not more worship

or awe, but a laughter we all rally
around, understood and needed joy,

made our own? If your acting
can't bear the burden, or demand

better representation, can you just walk away?
No one will fault you for that.

❧

Golden Shovel Suite

after Terrance Hayes

> *"I worry about my mind aestheticizing pain."*
> —Vanessa Angelica Villareal

> *"A poem could be the territory that makes the hurt beautiful."*
> —Phillip B. Williams

Variations of a River: a golden shovel for Ferguson

for Michael Brown/after Langston Hughes

1.

> *"To fling my arms wide/ In someplace of the sun/ To whirl and to dance/*
> *Till the white day is done/Then rest at cool evening beneath a tall tree/*
> *While night comes on gently/ Dark like me/That is my dream!"*
>
> –Langston Hughes

To the east, my river forms,
Fling-s from late summer blood, from
My dome to home. My
Arms can't break my fall, so this
Wide street, holds my body longer than it should.

In another time this might be
Some-thing as common as
Place-mats. In another time, this display
Of my body might find wind, or
The reef, or simply sink. But hours and hours of
Sun and sidewalk, my river can only cling

To camera. Waves of wetness
Whirl and lick the yellow radius
And then, anger forms, and then voices spread
To me and bounce, a sound better to
Dance and shake to, than to sleep:

> *I stand up with my hands up*
> *I put up, my hands up*
> *Then I'm spinnin' all my hands up*

Till the moment shatters through me, I'm
The fool in flip flops, a red cap, and
White socks. My hands full of the
Day I steal from a store. That dirt
Is mine to own. Pops says, what's
Done is gon get you one day, son. But

88

Then:— and now:— me at
Rest, watching my dark flow lurk about.
At least they could cover me. The summer night is
Cool-er than some think, chocolate
Evening frigid in red and blue. But
Beneath this place, this home of mine,
A small trickle of me is left, a
Tall tale of who I is remains: mountain,
Tree, gentle giant high as high water can get
While the dam is on lock. Let this
Night take me and not the man who
Comes here, scared and ready to put
On a shield to spray black bodies down.
Gently— if I gotta go, let it be the

Dark-ness my eyes got, cherry
Like with a pit of apology. Blood leaving
Me, wandering back to

That place where I first believed.
Is that you, dear Lord, or you, sweet mama? Tell
My homies don't be drawn to the current of a 40. Avoid the
Dream of this slow moving river.

2.
"To fling my arms wide/ In the face of the sun,/ Dance! Whirl! Whirl!
Till the quick day is done./ Rest at pale evening . . ./
A tall, slim tree . . ./ Night coming tenderly/ Black like me."
                                                    –Langston Hughes

This singing to-
o; this swaying, fling-
ing jazz and gospel: my
poetry, my arms
open wide

for you, big boy. In-
sert my words into the
defeat of your eyes and face.
The foolishness of
a boy is just that—: yet the-
y steal they sun

out of you and take any dance
you have left. I wish for whirl
and rejoicing, but the dusk is a whirl

tempting you till
morning becomes the
mourning of black souls. How quick
can I steady your day
with a word, with th-is
lingering music? The blues done

got you now. Rest
here. Lay down the law at

the crease of my poems, not the pale
promise of a dying justice. Evening

is a heavy log moving steadily toward a-
nger, drifting towards the last words a tall
boy might float down a slim
river. I have carved hymns into a tree

before. I have seen the night
arbor offer us nothing but ropes. This coming
age is that discordant. This age is not tenderly

embracing our bodies, but dear son, your black
body has a lyric for the moonlight like
an aria, like an orchestrated couplet, like me.

Eric Garner's Last Gasp: a golden shovel love poem
for Eric and Esaw Garner

*"Every time you see me, you want to mess with me. I'm tired of it. It stops
today. I'm minding my own business. Please just leave me alone. I told
you the last time, please just leave me alone. Please don't touch me. Don't
touch me. I can't breathe..."* –Eric Garner

"Joy is an act of resistance." –Toi Derricot

This light, this wide light I
make it to, home. I can't
wait for you to join. Sweet Wife, let's breathe

turquoise into this stillness. Every
inch of its glow, the time
we first met. What do you
recall? I remember see-
ing velvet hair spring, a me-

ssage telling me to pursue, an i-
nvitation for dates then kisses— *can't
get close enough.* When I breathe

into our first night alone, you
closed your eyes, want-
ing the expanse of a night to-
gether to hold black love. We was a mess
all over the room— we, turn turquoise with
black between sheets. *Just Me*

and You crooning, *Don't worry 'bout a damn thang.* I
sing across your shoulders, down your back. "Can't
leave yet," you say :: "spend your every breath-

ing life with me. Dearest I'm
yours." I keep the past fresh not my tired

91

body when the officers bring all of
me to the cement. My body, not theirs to handle, none it.

Like a piece of fruit, like the loosies I
sell, I am singled out. They want to cant-
aloup me, thump me down until ripe. Breath-

ing a vicious red when they question, I go flat. But it
ain't what lays me down, darlin' Esaw. What stops
me, what boulders me down today

and yesterday and all the days i-
n between our first meeting, has been you. I can't
give them my life or leisure. I breathe

your love, tell them: take the hustle, take what I'm
doing and put it in a box so it stops re-minding
them that wrong is happening— I tell them my
sins are that miniscule. We all have dirty business
to store away. The box says, "I'm obeying, officer,

but are you listening?" *Don't worry bout a damn thang*, I
hear you crooning. Baby, bringing me back. Can't
give them you. Won't allow them to breathe

illness to your good nature— love, you golden to the river. Please
believe, I quantify all your worth— I counts good, damnit! *Just
me and you,* turquoise and the moon, too. We'll leave
this world behind. We'll step off towards the west. Hang our me-
ager hopes from a bumper, go out alone.

I can't think right now, but I-
'm sure we 'gon be alright. God's plans can't
be broken, or choked to the point breath-

ing stops. Nah, babe, ain't going out like that. I
have to tell you about the towers here. Haven't told
you about the music skimming off the clouds. You

have yet to see how your boy got wings, the
real big ones I always told you I wanted. At last,
I can just coast, just glide on by to check on you from time to time.

I leave you with nine mouths to wash, wake and i-
nstitute. Get them before they get you, honey. Can't
let weeds run wild. Teach them how to breathe

to the tune only home makes. Please,
babe, they'll need all your ears and back, too. Just-
ice might be blind, but you shouldn't be. If you leave
my smile with them, if you jot down a phrase or two from me,
then I'm there to help. You won't be alone.

Evening is on its way. Here, stars jet so close, I
swear I can grab one, for you, just in case you can't
get here for a minute. Take all the time you need. Breathe.

Please breathe. Remember turquoise, and please
take it in. Feel it all through your chest— don't
cough it away. It's trying to touch
me, too, babe. Teaching me

how to flow with it. How to fly i-
n the face of fools who can't
ever be this alive. I breathe

living memories that don't
fade, or ever let cops touch.
I drift on turquoise, reminding me,

as I wait for you, love: I
am the flow that can't
help but breathe.

A Prayer for Living Onward: a golden shovel for the nine victims of Emanuel AME

"They died between the sacred walls of the church of God,
and they were discussing the eternal meaning of love.
This stands out as a beautiful, beautiful thing for all generations."
–Dr. Martin Luther King

By the time the heat of this settles, they
will still be gone, yet I want to know they died
fearlessly. I want there to be no blood or stone between
their bible verses or their names each must have offered to the
new comer. I want to believe there was no malice while the sacred
hour of prayer was happening but the walls
of a church, this sanctuary, have become the streets of
Baltimore or Ferguson or Sanford. The
path my belief wants to take is on fire. Burns with church
bombings from the past, riots in Watts, the insurrection of
Denmark Vesey, and yet all I muster up is: Dear God,

Not again. By the time the heat of this settles, and
authorities cry and try to keep cool, nine will still be gone. They
deserve blood, my mind keeps saying but the Reverend knows they were
praying long after the others were finished. He knows discussing
the ways of God living amongst the unsung heroes of the
community takes time. All truth, but so was Vesey's path to the eternal.
His anger broods in my veins. He understood how meaning
can be shrouded in the preparation for an uprising, that the people of
the community need their fists to accompany their wits. But love

back then, as now it is now, was stronger, and this
is what the Reverend keeps reminding me, and what stands
in the way of my foolishness. The Reverend knows that noise is out
everywhere, always has been. It is a rampage as quick as sin, and as
old, too. The thick waters surrounding Charleston, are a
reminder of this. This boy cannot strike down the beautiful

folks whose struggle built these walls. This beautiful
church is not a museum. And we are not its relics, a thing
to be dusted and preserved, a thing to be forgotten. Forego the anger for
another time. And when I nod, he knows the fight crescendos, all
of it, as I go to my knees the way his kind has done for generations.

Cherish these Days
After Sade/for Honzek

You're ruling the way that I move/And I breathe your air/You only can rescue me/You show me how deep love can be/This is my prayer –Sade

To the boy who pulls my son back to life, you're
all reflexes, and quick grace amongst the ruling
arrangements of living: deep breath, the-
n exhale, deep breath, then exhale. These way-
s, stitched into the seam of your surfer nature so that
the moment within a water tunnel is optimized, appreciated. I
long for this sight, but never for the vision of my son, his move

while driving— towards edge and wreck, his body in full seizure and
not a swell, but swerve. All I can imagine, the only thought I
envision: shredded metal. But there you are, demanding: Breathe.
Breathe. Breathe. There you are, barrel breaking into the worst water your
life has presented. With no way to bail out, you offer my son air.

You don't give in or run away, the
only one there to deliver him back. I hope you
can understand how you've
rescue-d me, too from this wipe and washout. Rinsed
me clean, and my son back to feet.

Ode to the boy who pulls my son back to life, you
carry every cell I vibrate, all the blood and bones too, show
me how to ride the waves worry, show me
how ease is a sunrise mirroring off the ocean's skin, how
a cutback is the surfer's way to reposition life into a life: deep
breath, then exhale. Deep breath, then exhale. A parent's love
can crest and white into foam on top of a child's seas. Can
be deep water drowning them too. But boy, you be

This life giving friendship. You, h-
is partner on this journey, so
my offering: be our family, and let our
prayer-s cherish any and all of your days.

Love Letter from George Clinton to Bruno Mars: an imagined conversation

after Marcus Wicker

Yes, I said it
to you, brother.

Said with or
without auto-tune

my ode has love
all through the teeth.

Don't believe me— just
watch the way I kiss

ego, and curl praise: your silk
and links blow the breaks off

a Caddy, to the stars, a shine
so funky, where my shoes,

where my spray? Dot a dimple,
spark a smile so when the bass

whomp-whomps we all pause
on you. Yes, brother Bruno, fly on.

But can I preach one time:
ass and all its shimmer will go

limp and so will dancing dudes,
their suffocating swag & strut

gone to the wash. Not tryna
hate, just don't want

history hustling out
on the wrong horse, you dig?

This funk nation was built on the backs
of those who needed voice,

so put your pinky
in your pocket, and listen.

Listen past glitz and champagne
flutes clicking to the moon.

Past applause and booties,
too— overcome that hump.

Get down to the stank,
the gap growing between

a sidewalk and middle
of the street. I'm talking

about threshold, about consciousness
reaching that intermediate height

a party and protest grooves for:
man, they killing us in the streets.

We are the endangered species
of all eras and areas, and the down

stroke you wield, most uptown folks
can't understand. Look out

to the masses chanting the polish
of your name— not every soul wants

Versace-patent-leather. Illumination
can't be the unaffordable 'fit. So

when you donkey chain
a bright horizon around

your neck, use it to take
away blight and shade.

Not tryna rain on your burning
roof, baby bubba—these folks here

to see the dip in your hips,
your glide, and not your snide.

I just want your noise
to put us on the one again.

Feed us marshmallow
yams, but butter up the knowledge

baby, so when you cue:
watch—me—break—it—down—

we to the rim like full,
like your bad-self, *like (uh).*

Alternative Language for Transformation
for Monika and Traci

Not tangled blood—no knots morphing and
        clinging cells to shear the cat

Not tissue

No percentages, no rates
        nor a scale to kick around

No feet to shoot pink ribbons

Not a bowed head anywhere
        to hang, hurt, or remove

No, you're not dead meat, not made up
        or in line for a make over

And even though you like it, no
        need for oil or back rubs

There will not be a pepper tree full
        of juju, or voodoo forests of free doses

No séance or prayers sent
        to stone or hard ears

Not officer-kick-this-habit

Not a thief tip-toeing, hands wet
        with wrong

And no, not a warrior, their victories
        and defeats— both measured by destruction

When you transform,
        in this world, in this now—

The violence in your blood
        becomes two birds

Protecting a vision of what ought to be

Two birds, singing on both sides of your back— a tattoo

The right forms wings
        as pointed teeth

Ingesting the grace,
        inhaling the good take

Ink in flight and
        feather on the left

Spreading to the sunrise— over
        shoulder, and straight to the heart

O heart, send the soldiers
        to their downhill homes

So two birds can harmonize

Not a in fugue nor the blues—
        a wail won't do

Not in fear or mere invention

Two birds sing their bodies clean

Sing the kill away, and take
        the stones their rebel cells wield

Sing seeds and expansion, fields
        of faith waving as far as the eye can see

IV. Her, Gone

Portrait of Harriet Tubman as a Stone

Tubman Panel 19

Harriet:— rock, hard hands,
worn from digging or carrying

black bodies, or clawing
black bodies to hurry, or quieting
black bodies when the patrol is close

enough to break spirits, hardness points
worried souls north.

And Harriet:— stone face, enduring
any hurt winter has to offer. Here, shine
is polished black. Your eyes, in two

directions: *just-in-case.* Not all
passages are a doorway toward safety,

tunnels headed to liberty's light.
Harriet, your stone surges,
and your gaze bolders each

way. Whether you lead us up or
around a mountain, it will avoid

what hate hurls.
Your shoulders, covered in dark
linen, your head wrapped

in cloth, but somewhere underneath
a rifle waits. A cherry pit bullet

poised and in position: *just-in-case.*
You remind. *If we a stones throw away
from freedom, imma get you there.*

Douglass to Tubman :: an Erasure

Rochester, August 29, 1868

Dear Harriet:

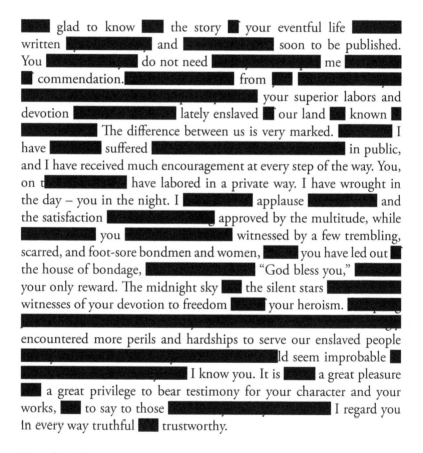

████ glad to know ██ the story █ your eventful life ██████
written █████████ and █████████████ soon to be published.
You █████████ do not need ██████████ me █████████
█ commendation. ████████████████ from ██ █████████████
██████████████████████████████ your superior labors and
devotion ████████████ lately enslaved █ our land ██ known █
█████████ The difference between us is very marked. ████████ I
have █████ suffered █████████████████████████ in public,
and I have received much encouragement at every step of the way. You,
on t██████████ have labored in a private way. I have wrought in
the day – you in the night. I █████████ applause █████████ and
the satisfaction ██████████████ approved by the multitude, while
████████████ you ███████████ witnessed by a few trembling,
scarred, and foot-sore bondmen and women, █████ you have led out █
the house of bondage, ████████████ "God bless you," ████████
your only reward. The midnight sky ██ the silent stars █████████
witnesses of your devotion to freedom █████ your heroism. ████████
██
encountered more perils and hardships to serve our enslaved people
████████████████████████ld seem improbable █
████████████████████ I know you. It is █████ a great pleasure
████ a great privilege to bear testimony for your character and your
works, ████ to say to those ██████████████████████ I regard you
In every way truthful ████ trustworthy.

Your friend,

F████ D█████.

Brown to Browne :: Douglass to Tubman Remix
for Mahogany Browne

New York, July 1, 2016

Dear Browne:

I know the story of your life
has written labors,
and you have been marked

to speak on the suffering
in public, and of the little justice
our folks have received.

No time for encouragement,
every step I have labored
has been private, but you need me

wrought in the day— you, be an anvil
pounding night to no applause.
You say, ain't no satisfaction, when

multitudes be trembling scarred,
and foot-sore. Black men and women,
trapped in a house of bondage.

These black bodies are not food
for thought. They are not creative inspiration—
You know I have plenty to talk

about: fatherhood and such. You say, words
be my only reward for those struck down
before their songs had time to spring forth.

So let me bring the midnight sky, so the silent
stars beatbox and hum. Show me how devotion
be a rattle, be your freedom from the tongue.

Heroism, all theirs, encountered perils and
hardships, a service for our people. Yes, we
be the living with great privilege to bear

our people's testimony and character.
Let them run through our works,
leading us, and I will regard your everyway

truthful, trustworthy. I'll gather the gold,
you carry the gun. Browne, I will be your dearest
friend, and companion in this war.

Onward

for Amanda Johnston/after Jay-Z and Pharrell

Tubman Panel 10

Here— a canopy of night, and here, your broken
Chains, shattered shackles you stock
For the journey— nothing wasted while North
Beckons. The dazzling stars friend and find you
Modest, wanting. But you radiate, not a weary bone
In your body, *just a red bag & my blood.*

I'm a hustler baby, I just want you to know.
        It ain't where I been, but where I'm 'bout to go.

Here— a crag to contain, and a mountain
To blister your grip. Here— a weed to wrangle
Steps, creeping vines, thick with thorns to tear
Into your feet. Dirt muddled with tracks of flesh.
If not careful, they'll come for me— They'll slither & strike
Me down. Sweet Harriet, your thoughts cannot give,
Cannot succumb to green or to river. A wall
Of rocks— the unyielding you learn from.
Their hardness all I need to hold.

I'm a hustler baby, I just want you to know.
        It ain't where I been, but where I'm 'bout to go.

Here she be, Lord, all twenty five years of her
For your sky to behold, a squint of energy
Swirling about, like a child— a free child

Amongst streaked blue night. The Good God air
Is a finger calling forth, reaching towards while
Harriet's grace gestures— *I be gone, onward.*

I'm a hustler baby, I just want you to know.
        It ain't where I been, but where I'm 'bout to go.

Study

Tubman Panel 16

Our future
selves believe
she be in
a hurry,
gone fast
through trees
and dirt, be dark on
the dark night.
Feet up
and running.
Streaks of black folks
carrying the little
they own in sacks.
Black folks in burlap,
huddled tight—
tight as forests
covering escape routes.
Their souls riding
on their soles.
Harriet, gone
ahead, leading without
a light to guide.
But she studied
the lands, know'd
the woods.
Man-made maps
tattooed on her
belly, stretched
the way a newborn
do. A branch
of marks across her—
be safety,
be water for hours,

be a kind smile
and the smell
of food. Our future
selves, blind
to this deliberate path
Sister Harriet cleaves.

Frederick Douglass Dreams of Harriet
after Roger Reeves

Tubman Panel 20: Post-Fugitive Slave Act 1850

Forget flesh— forget sickness,
and the cold that too, has a cold.
You hope to dry her wet clothes,
her skirts dragging wet from the pinky toe
of Southern Illinois all the way up
into Canada, home of snow and so much more
snow. Mr. Douglass, this white everywhere, no need
for witnesses, law has us all running
from white to white. Ol' Harriet wrings Lake Michigan
into Lake Huron, mixes a tinge of blood
to have hounds every which way
the current flows— too goddamn close
the last time. Have you forgotten
how teeth teach you how to hustle?
Surely *you* know she keeps a bullet lodged
between her gums & lips so not to yell
at slow pokes. Her single file pace
conceals tracks, a hidden avenue freedom marches
on, daily. No time for rehearsal— only the routine
of living, constant as Canada's wide
arms. You know she will eat in silence
but whistles a wren song throughout
the miles—: Black folks need music
no matter the situation, no matter how many frozen
mounds stand in our way, or how many frozen minds
pass a bogus law. Mr. Douglass, when in front
of enough money to support escapes,
Tune your heart to this verse:—
never going back without returning with a few more.
Harriet belongs to them, rather than some
place. If she stops to huddle, most times folks
need to breathe or drink. Can your dream become

the speech watching them drinking what
her eyes offer? Can a crowd to forget their privilege
to sense the distance traveled when you tell them
fate is not slender— no one dying on black trees,
thin arms and nothing to supply? Fate is vast
as Canada's storm ridden sky— a crystal heaven
sheltering from the harm south spawns.

Pieta Ghazal: Harriet Tubman Mourns for Freddie Gray

for Freddie Gray

Tubman Panel 29

I return to deliver a hurt clean—
I come to lay a boy to rest— His clean,

Sparks, yanks me from the past— I'm vibrant,
Again— an angel caressing him into a clean

Baby sleep— Yes, Lawd, *again*, I'm the one guiding
Saints— I knows which roots will heal a boy, clean—

Knows all kinds of elusive, elixirs to turn women into tiptoe-
Fog-whisper— My herbs had men ghost-walking clean

Through fortress walls, damn its thickness— Worked,
So this boy could stitch freedom on his sleeve— clean—

O sweet Baltimore boy, did you bring me back for
Tricks & chats, 'cuz I can't conjure a clean

Pulse in you— This resurrection, too
Late to save, restoring the clean

Merit of our folks— Too late for fear to strike out
And stunt your bolt, so I'm left with this clean

Option: Be Moses of the drift, pulled here to lead you home—
Here to soothe and sing you clean— honorably clean

Ghazal between Icons: an imagined conversation
for Freddie Gray

> *"Going to live at Baltimore, laid the foundation, and opened*
> *the gateway, to all my subsequent prosperity."*
> *—Frederick Douglass*

Douglass Panel 32

US flag, never half mast for you, black Baltimore Boy
Red stripes match my red shirt— portrait of a black Baltimore boy.

Son of red brick and Westside, been with you in these blood beaten Streets.
"Privileged men" nearly gouge the eyes out of me, a black Baltimore boy.

I scream streaks, 33 minutes of cries and a lonely road. Unrelenting
Field swallowing the air of a black Baltimore boy.

The news wraps you in lists, trying to destroy the light of your name,
Waxing moon sliver of light— metaphor for black Baltimore boys?

Some say: new moon is you turning in your grave. Others say: new moon when we
Together. We a dark so stone thick, they name it: Black-ass Baltimore Boys.

Son, I yearn to know things have changed. Tell me our black shines gold.
Tell me I paved nothing but golden tulips for all blacks, dear Baltimore boy.

US flag, stem and post, higher than sea breeze, but not my goals.
Because of you, my dreams sky high— Imma proud black Baltimore boy.

No more silence for you. Our names sing a stargazed funk. Even in
Similar sleep, our rest— proper tunes and beats for black Baltimore boys.

Mr. Douglass, none of us die in vain, right? You— the lion who makes that truth.
Freddie, blue haze-heaven awaits. Beautiful as black and you, Baltimore boy.

Face to Face: Lawrence and the Douglass Death Mask

Douglass Panel 30

Feel the comb, the scissors shearing
Your goat-colored hair. Feel Mr. Dunbar
Lathering your face with rubber, and

Petroleum jelly tears. He cries into the salve
On your face and fight. He rubs you opal
So not to scrub the eloquence off your skin.

Your swollen mouth still chewing chains
Or chewing granite. Your mouth, full of the print
From last night's speech, wants to rebuff:

Do you mean to lock me in plaster?
Do you mean to cripple this posture?
This death is mine to own and preserve.

Your skin, no longer slavery's dockyard
Nor it's blistering cannons. No longer the bright
Brown of a town hall's pews. Your mask, white

And crusted, will stiffen into accomplishment,
Into hallmark, into a lion's thick hide
And heavy muscle. When the funeral beckons,

Your stern face will startle the church's nave
Until the guise rests in your home, in the hallway
Near your swift and quiet collapse.

O Frederick Douglass, Come home and settle,
With a body, a pipe, and chuckle for your dear
Miss Pitts. Rock back and forth so the floor planks

Creak as your foot taps an anthem. To the seascape,
To the searchlight, the beat guiding your first wife.
She waits with your mother on a road the ice and chill

Of this country cannot reach. This death mask, holds
Your self-made life and labor, validates the extremes
Of *manhood*, and dignifies your slumber.

We : Invent : We

after Terry Wolverton

> *we-be/be-bent E-ben-glish,/em-bem-bra-baced i-bit/*
> *the-ben e-be-ra-based- i-bit/ a-bat the-be sa-bame ti-bime.*
> *—Robin Coste Lewis*

1. Quake Swarm

We tell ourselves: solid
We think trillions of forms
We point to shrines, invent
       ourselves the planet in place
We are convinced our matter holds
       everything we cling to

But like Yoko Ono vibrates: "Everything is shaking"

We're really set in motion together
We're frequency, all the time
       energy shaking delusion and fixed mythologies
We make fervor— musical
We're one giant quake
       a swarm of tenacious breath:
We matter
We are song

"Everything is shaking"

We : vibrate Yoko Ono
We : cling to everything
We : hold the planet in place
We : invent : We
We : trillions of forms
We : ourselves— solid

2. Ransack yourself where you stand

We : junk piles
We : dust heap

I lean into myself
Hold this detritus

A late empire settled thick
Layers in us all

Experienced— Boxed—
Unsorted— Toppling

In the Sixties they said:
In case of nuclear war

Bend over,
Kiss your ass goodbye

But isn't that just shelter
Duck and cover

Tells me how to contain
Unfiled Atrocities

Tells me
We : can't have this place

Tells me
We : can't find anything that used be

3. After Acres of Skin: the history of medical experiments on Black prisoners after Allen M. Hornblum

History   :
Science   :

                 Not recorded in the usual tomes

                 whispered in screams across unending nights

                 all conducted in the name of—

History   :
Science   :

                 It's erasure

                 it's curiosity— cruelty

                 passed down to successive generations of—

History   :
Science   :

                 It's pretense of objectivity

                 of discussion

                 of genes— not

History   :
Science   :

                 When forced to stop the experiments

History   :
Science   :

                refused to look into the eyes

                Black prisoners no more real to—
History   :
Science   :

                than the research

                taken on animals

4. Sometimes Noise

We : the clanking machinery of thought

We : the factory of heartbeats— 24-hour shifts
        lit up with fire

Our noise— better than the silence piercing
        us like tomorrow's bad news

Our dilapidated druthers— better than
        fetid winds and its shut down bitterness

We : rather have our engines on—
        noise sucking the cells out of work

We : the irregular factory
        surrounding hillsides

And sometimes we: the rain

And sometimes we: the breath
        left on porches

What can cover all that

Love Letter to Rashida Jones
after Marcus Wicker

dear dear Rashida   I could spend
the next three days browsing

through images of just your hair
½ white ½ black strands of kindness:—

brunette streaks by day turned slang at primetime
but this would be mere fandom   and what I need

is advice for my daughter who is all
cherry coke and a pack of bubble gum

all dust and chipped fingernails
I imagine she is you at twelve discretely claiming

all parts Peggy and Quincy:—caramel freckles
between a disarray of pre-teened brows

what my daughter knows of herself
she loves both the fight and funk found in her

unsettling curls she coils into a nest
of family stories made calm by water or tears

like your name she knows she can't hide
what makes her   *I'm ethnic* you have said

to an industry that buys itself tan brushing away
both your white and black-ness   she gets this

she gets your ease when correcting negligence
she gets that it could be a simple hand waving

across sand and stone   it can be as slight
as good manners   dearest Rashida like you her smile

could correct any ignorance   but I know it
takes more than tricks and magic for a walnut

and honey skinned girl whose half & half blood
swirls through my coffee dark skin and at times

away from it   will she wince when we talk
about lynchings or Tupac or Sandra Bland

will she know they were not accidents
or causalities of a quiet war   what is being waged

against her blood is as loud as genocide
my responsibility is not an empty basket

I'm only asking because she's close
to turning us off just to see your syndicated smile

glow from house to house   when she speaks
of you she verifies your facts to hers

she dreams they are a dandelion away
I know this is supposed to be a love letter

and so I'll beg:—I need you Rashida
please tell her that black bodies are a blessing

like rain—:

like cinnamon—:

like Tupac and Sandra Bland

Re-Portrait Your Name, Douglas
after Earth, Wind, & Fire

Slip into your father's
Downstairs lounge, not

To gamble— even though
Any given 1998 Friday, folks

Would have gathered pensions
Or paychecks, hugged up

To E&J or Bud Lights, some
Smoke— cigs or blunts,

Some Stevie, some Earth,
Wind & Fire, a ballgame

Or two, just to let spirits spirit
The week's end— *finally.*

Go deep down into this
Memory. Folks and more

Folks in recollection but also in
The way of [*the reasons that we're*

Here]: your pops and his picture
Wall— photos of the abundant

And alive (even if the captured are not),
Each speaks theatrical, orchestral:

[*La—La La La La—La— La La La La*].
Your mind sways and claps with every

Image cast. These pictures,
Each a singular achievement for

Black America. From floor to cciling
No speeches, no marching,

No aches or goddamn tears. Only
One scholar to speak of, and he is carrying

A plate of ribs, greens and cornbread,
So, no pretense either. Full length

Portraits of everyday freedom, laughter.
Scorn and malice— not gone,

But the hardships slashed or ripped
Away— too heavy for this wall to hold.

And now memory creeps toward
Imagination: Frederick Douglass

Shoulder to shoulder with you.
His daring apparition surveying

His yield, his hard doing. What will he see?
Valor in afros? Versions of Black

Folks in collage? Does he notice
Our variance over the years? Our range

Of joy, people being comfortably black,
Honest— as dependable as black

Can be when fixed by a camera's flash?
After you tell him, *we can smile now,*

Dream your pops offering advice
And a brew: *Leave his ass here. We be*

Aight. Two Freds tight in their
Radiance, in their adjacent delight.

Two Freds acknowledge how
Close *fruition* is, and grant the claim

On *Douglas*, and *duty*, as yours.

The Free Life
after Tracy K. Smith

When some folks talk of freedom
They speak as if it is the glorious outside
When weather sun-kisses our shoulders, and
Pitchers stay full of bright fruit and cucumber
Laughter, sisters and brothers in a backyard, pops
At the pit, mom— all apron and head wrap, mixing
Potato salad, my kids dancing to P-funk or head-knocking to
Ice Cube—: yes, the good day, with love on my lap,
Her hand on my heart as I look to the sky— the distances
Between any of us, falling off the bone, so far and away.

∾

Bibliography and Primary Texts

Douglass, Frederick, and William L. Garrison. *Narrative of the Life of Frederick Douglass, an American Slave*. England: Wortley. Printed by Joseph Barker, 1846. Print.

---. ed James M. C. Smith. *My Bondage and My Freedom*. New York: Miller, Orton & Mulligan, 1855. Print.

---. *The Life and Times of Frederick Douglass: From 1817-1882, written by himself,* with an Introduction by the Right Hon. John Bright, ed. John Lobb. London: Christian Age Office, 1882. Print.

McDuffie, Dwayne, *Icon: A Hero's Welcome,* Vol. 1. Burbank: Milestone-DC Comics. 2009. Print.

---. *Icon: The Mothership Connection,* Vol. 2. Burbank: Milestone-DC Comics. 2010. Print.

Stauffer, John, Zoe Trodd, Celeste-Marie Bernier, Henry L. Gates, and Kenneth B. Morris. *Picturing Frederick Douglass: An Illustrated Biography of the Nineteenth Century's Most Photographed American*. New York: Liveright. 2015. Print.

Wheat, Ellen Harkins. *Jacob Lawrence: The Frederick Douglass and Harriet Tubman Series of 1938-1940*. Seattle: University of Washington Press, 1991. Print.

❧

Author's Notes

Icon is a biographical/poetic reflection, using ekphrasis to weave a narrative. Contextual notes, references, and links to the paintings can be found on the author's website: www.fdouglasbrown.com.

Despite the resemblance to an image the words might have taken, each of the poems marked "Daguerreotype," "Douglass Panel" or "Tubman Panel," are composites from either a Frederick Douglass photograph, one of the corresponding Jacob Lawrence paintings, and/or a selection from one of three Frederick Douglass's books (see the bibliography for full text citation). Except when noted, I have written and developed all of the poems.

Lastly, readers will notice the deliberate omission of any poems that explore the relationships Frederick Douglass had with Abraham Lincoln, John Brown, Martin R. Delany, both of his wives, Anna Murray and Helen Pitts, his mistress, or any of his children. Poems interrogating these relationships will find themselves in subsequent books.

Acknowledgements

With ineffable love and gratitude, first for my remarkable partner, Claire, and my children: Isaiah, Olivia, Simone; then to blood family: Ahna, Darius, Derek, Lil John, Monika, Sherry, Katie, Dave (and a host of nieces & nephews); and finally, Cave Canem and Kundiman, my ink families.

Undying respect and thanks to the Accomplices: Chiwan Choi, Judeth Oden-Choi, Peter Woods of Writ Large Press; Janice Lee of Entropy; Michael Seidlinge of Civil Coping Mechanisms.

Love to those who have inspired this work directly, and pulled it along when I didn't think I could: Jamal Adams, Tara Betts, Sara Borjas, Mahogany Browne, Rocio Carlos, Jessica Ceballos, Lisa Cheby, Cathy Lin Che, Chiyuma Elliott, Doug Emmanuel, Ralph Eubanks, Amanda Fletcher and PEN Center USA, Ángel García, Natalie J. Graham, Peter J. Harris, Terrance Hayes, Jen Hofer, Ashaki M. Jackson, Zachary Jensen, Tyehimba Jess, Amanda Johnston, Dae Jung, Rachel Kaminer, Traci Kato-Kiriyama, Douglas Kearney, Jacob Kelly, Doug Knot, Robin Coste Lewis, Nate Marshall, Marisa Matarazzo, Tom Marsh, Victoria Lynn McCoy, Andrew McFadyen-Ketchum, Danielle Mitchell, Rebecca Norton, Regis Armani Peeples, Cassandra Powers, Umar "Frohawk Two Feathers" Rashid, Jesse Rodriguez, Luis Rodriguez, Joseph Rios, Nicole Sealey, Cheyanne Sauter and the Art Share LA crew, Jeffrey Schultz, Wyatt Underwood, Geoff Walker, Maya Washington, Terry Wolverton, Phillip B. Williams, Brittany Williams, John Vella, Chad Yates, Jake Young.

Special Thanks to the extra milers for their kind and tough words, pep talks and real talk, their keen vision when I had none: Jeff Adkins, Jaswinder Bolina, Geffrey Davis, Lee Harrick, Kimko Hahn, Patrick Rosal, The SGV Crew, Mike Sonksen, Cate Lycurgus, Michael Douglas McElhinney.

Rest In Power Hermia, Freddie B., Phil, and Monica Hand…this dream of excellence has your names on it.

I am honored to gratefully acknowledge the editors and staff of the following publications in which these poems first appeared, some in early drafts and titles.

Angel City Review – "olemrauldsaythisthegospeltruththatifyouteachthatniggertoreadtherebenokeepinghim,andthaswhutmakemewoki'swoktowriteantoread: ghazal"

Angel's Flight Literary West – "Pieta Ghazal: Harriet Tubman Mourns Freddie Gray"; "Ghazal between Icons: an imagined conversation"; "Onward"

Bat City Review – "Darkness, My Mother"

Black Renaissance Noire – "Daguerreotype: c. 1841"; "Planation Tour :: how a painting happens"; Daguerreotype: c. 1843"; "Imagining Lawrence Imagine the 11th of August 1841"

Cave Canem Anthology XIV: Poems 2012-2013 – "Go Fo"

Chaparral – "What I mean When I say Begotten"; "Second Sleep"

Chicago Quarterly Review – "Mr. Covey, Shall We Dance?"; "Sermon in Nantucket: Garrison Commissions Douglass"; "A Prayer for Living Onward: a golden shovel for the nine victims of Emanuel AME"

Coiled Serpent Anthology – "Love Letter to Rashida Jones"

Entropy Magazine – "We : Invent : We"; "Anthem Kundiman: Work"

The Normal School – "Re-Portrait as a Muslim Boy :: Beg. Borrow. Steal."

Southern Humanities Review – "Variations of a River: a golden shovel for Ferguson"

Toe Good Poetry – "Free Hymns"

Vinyl – "Poem My Mother Doesn't Want Right Now"

Virginia Quarterly Review – "Begotten :: February 1818"; "The Flogging"; "Face to Face: Lawrence and the Douglass Death Mask"

Wherewithal – "A Slave Boy's Lullaby"; "Up Jump the Funk Never Felt This Bad"

OFFICIAL

CCM ●

GET OUT OF JAIL
* VOUCHER *

- -

Tear this out.

Skip that social event.

It's okay.

You don't have to go if you don't want to. Pick up
the book you just bought. Open to the first page.
You'll thank us by the third paragraph.

If friends ask why you were a no-show, show them
this voucher.

You'll be fine.

- -

We're coping.

●